Hebron Church of Christ Library

194

T4-APU-158

99 PLUS ONE

99 PLUS ONE
Copyright 1971 The Tree House
Library of Congress Catalog Card No. 72-135225
International Standard Book No. 0-8066-1108-1
All rights reserved

Manufactured in the United States of America

 A TREE HOUSE PRODUCTION

99 PLUS ONE

STORY BY
GERARD A. POTTEBAUM

ART BY
DANIEL E. JOHNSON

PUBLISHED BY
AUGSBURG PUBLISHING HOUSE
MINNEAPOLIS, MINNESOTA

One magnolia morning
a friend of the poor
took 100 children
to the city zoo.

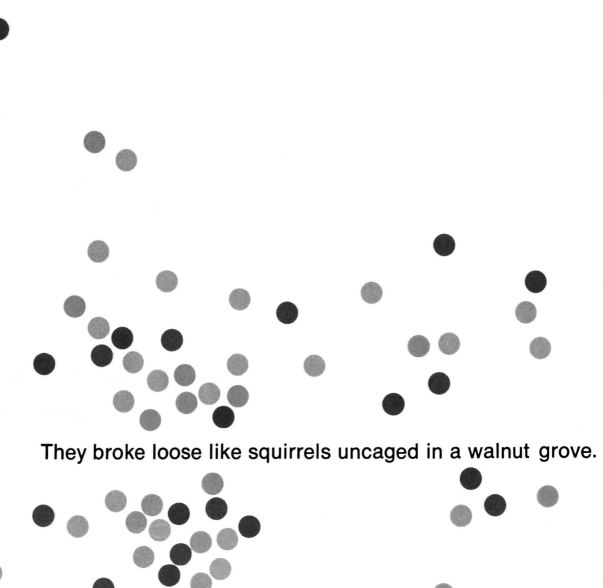

They broke loose like squirrels uncaged in a walnut grove.

They skipped and scampered to the monkeys swinging from bar to branch.

They wondered about the elephant drinking through his nose.

They tried to count the spots on the leopards . . .

. . . and the stripes on the zebras.

When the time came to go home
they gathered at the buses
and counted noses to see
that no one would be left behind.

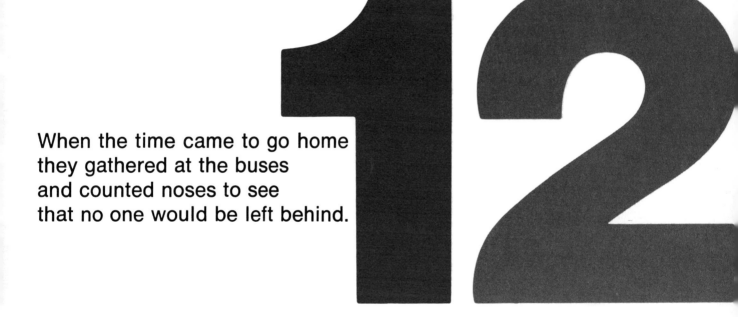

345

989

But when they finished counting,
their happy faces turned sad.
They could count only 99
when there should have been 100.

Someone was missing.

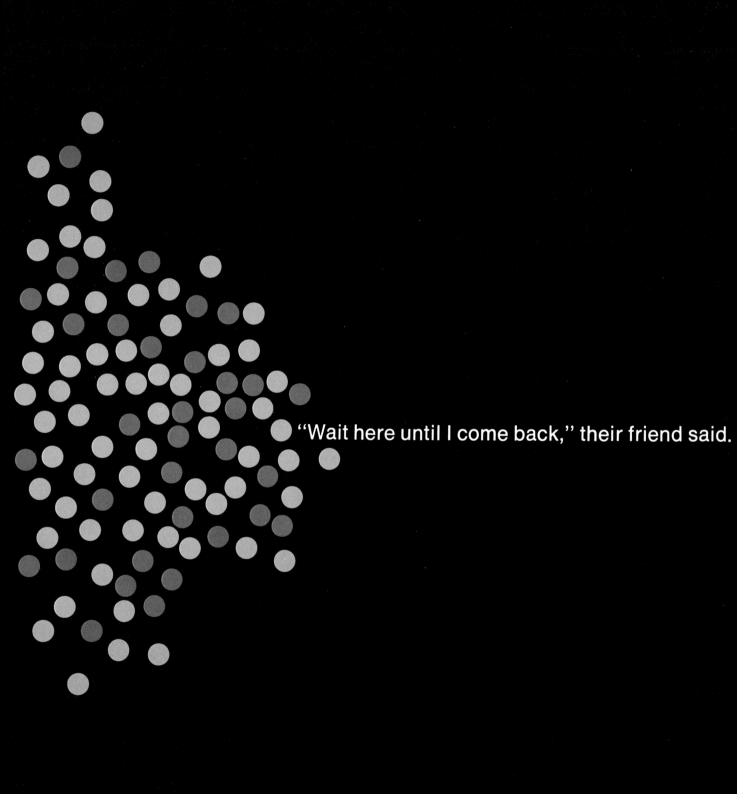

"Wait here until I come back," their friend said.

And he left the 99 to find the one who was lost.

He searched the pathways and cages .

. the benches and bushes.

. . .until at last he spotted the lost one crying dinosaur tears under a chestn

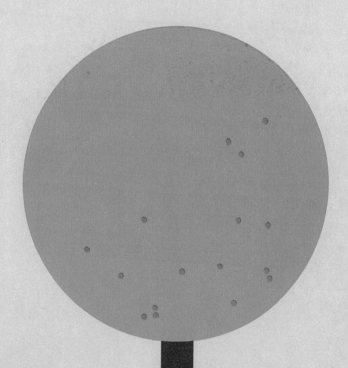

ee.   He ran to the child with a warm hug.

"This
son
to

. . . and carried him back to the ringing cheers of the 99.

sure is
nething
shout
about"

he said.

And so he bought them cones of their favorite flavors!

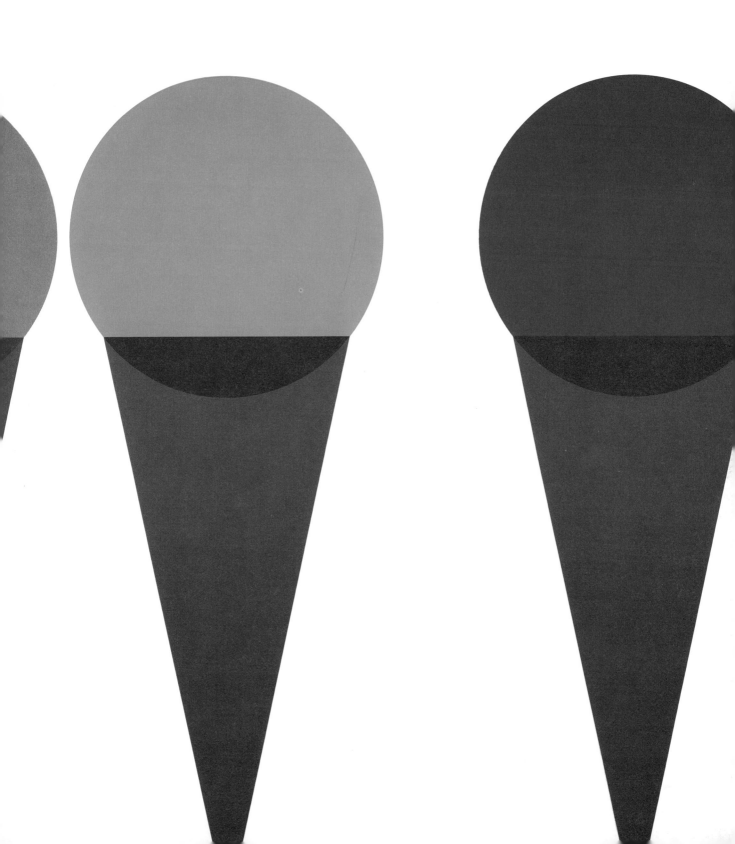

They were happier
over the one who was found
than over the 99
who were never lost.